THE ART OF
GAY LOVE

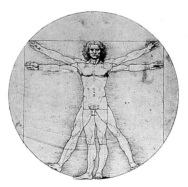

This edition first published in 1995 by Hamlyn,
an imprint of Reed Consumer Books Ltd,
Michelin House, 81 Fulham Road, London SW3 6RB
and Auckland, Melbourne, Singapore and Toronto.

Copyright © 1995 Reed International Books Limited
Introduction and extracts from work of Paul Keller,
David Rees and Robin Maugham © 1995 Peter Burton

ISBN 0 600 58744 4

A CIP catalogue record for this book is available from the British Library.

Produced by Mandarin Offset
Printed in Hong Kong

WARNING: With the prevalence of AIDS and other sexually
transmitted diseases, if you do not practise safe sex you
are risking your life and your partner's life.

Front cover: Miniature of a Young Man Against a Rose Tree,
Nicholas Hilliard, Victoria & Albert Museum, London
Back flap: David – *detail*,
Michelangeolo Buonarotti, Galleria dell'Accademia, Florence
Half title page: Vitruvian Man,
Leonardo da Vinci, Galleria dell'Accademia, Venice
Title page: Seated Bacchus,
Mano di Bastian Sbarri, Galleria Nazionale di Capodimonte, Naples
Page 4: The Mask of Tutankhamun – *detail showing eyes*,
Egyptian Museum, Cairo
Pages 6-7: Leonidas at Thermopylae, 480 B.C.,
Jacques Louis David, Louvre, Paris

THE ART OF
GAY LOVE

INTRODUCTION

$\mathcal{G}$ay love has been with us since the dawn of recorded history. Written or pictorial evidence exists from the earliest to the greatest civilizations. We know that men enjoyed sex with other men in the ancient civilizations of Babylonia, China, Egypt, Greece, India, Japan and Rome. Homosexuality existed in the New World – in the great city states of the Incas and Mayas as well as in the Indian tribes spread across the great plains of North America.

The relationship between Gilgamesh and Enkidu in the Babylonian *The Epic of Gilgamesh* – which dates from around 2000 B.C. – has caused that fragmentary work to be characterized in some quarters as the world's first gay novel.

According to some Egyptologists the heretic pharaoh Akhenaten shared an incestuous homosexual relationship with his brother and successor Smenkhkare. The Samurai, the powerful warrior class of Japan, were actively homosexual, frequently engaging in male-to-male relationships between a knight and his page in which the older served as a model and guide to the younger. The master and student relationship is found in the cultures of Greece and Rome as characterized in the epics of Homer, the philosophies of Socrates and Plato and the writing of Petronius (whose *The Satyricon* is another early gay fiction), Tacitus and Suetonius.

The literature of homosexuality is truly immense. Gay love has been a fit subject for exploration by playwrights and poets to autobiographers, biographers and novelists. Homosexual passion has been studied by doctors, scientists and sociologists and has been written about from perspectives romantic and analytical, taunting and titillating. Some of the greatest cultural influences have been creative gay men – and amongst those represented in this anthology are Michelangelo, Shakespeare, Goethe, Wilde and D.H. Lawrence. No more a love that dare not speak its name, gay love now declares itself proudly.

Why should I seek to ease intense desire
with still more tears and windy words of grief,
when heaven, or late or soon, sends no relief
to souls whom love hath robed around with fire?

Why need my aching heart to death aspire,
when all must die? Nay, death beyond belief
unto these eyes would be both sweet and brief,
since in my sum of woes all joys expire!

Therefore because I cannot shun the blow
I rather seek, say who must rule my breast,
Gliding between her gladness and her woe?

If only chains and bands can make me blest,
no marvel if alone and bare I go
an armed Knight's captive and slave confessed.

MICHELANGELO BUONARROTI
'To Tommaso de'Cavalieri', 16th century
(translated, John Addington Symonds)

Left: David – *detail*, Michelangelo Buonarroti,
Galleria dell'Accademia, Florence

His voice first attracted my attention, his countenance fixed it, and his manners attached me to him for ever ... I certainly love him more than any human being, and neither time nor distance have had the least effect on my (in general) changeable disposition.

GEORGE, LORD BYRON
to Miss Elizabeth Pigot,
writing about John Edleston,
5th July, 1807

Above: Portrait of Lord Byron,
19th century English School, The Fine Art Society, London
Right: Portrait of Lord Byron, Thomas Phillips

Shall I compare thee to a summer's day?
Thou art more lovely and more temperate:
Rough winds do shake the darling buds of May,
And summer's lease hath all too short a date:
Sometimes too hot the eye of heaven shines,
And often is his gold complexion dimm'd;
And every fair from fair sometimes declines,
By chance, or nature's changing course, untrimm'd;
But thy eternal summer shall not fade,
Nor lose possession of that fair thou ow'st;
Nor shall Death brag thou wander'st in his shade,
When in eternal lines to time thou grow'st:
So long as men can breathe, or eyes can see,
So long lives this, and this give life to thee.

WILLIAM SHAKESPEARE
'Sonnet 18', 16th century

Left: Miniature of a Young Man Against a Rose Tree,
Nicholas Hilliard, Victoria & Albert Museum, London

*Happy the moment when we are seated in the
palace, thou and I,
With two forms and with two figures, but with
one soul, thou and I.*

JALALU-DDIN RUMI
The Divani Shamsi Tabriz', 13th century
(translated, R.A. Nicholson)

Above and right: Illustration by Ian Beck in 'The Joy of Gay Sex'

Scarce had the morning starre hid from the light
Heavens crimson canopie with stars bespangled,
But I began to rue th' unhappy sight
Of that faire boy that had my hart intangled;
Cursing the time, the place, the sense, the sin;
I came, I saw, I viewed, I slipped in.

RICHARD BARNFIELD
'The Affectionate Shepheard', 16th century

Above: Young Man in a Black Cap and High Ruff,
Nicholas Hilliard, Victoria & Albert Museum, London

Only for my two loves' sake,
In whose love I pleasure take;
Only two do me delight
With their ever-pleasing sight;
Of all men to thee retaining
Grant me with these two remaining.

PHILIP SIDNEY
16th century

Above: Man Clasping Hand from a Cloud, possibly William Shakespeare,
Nicholas Hilliard, Victoria & Albert Museum, London

Gabriel stretched out his arms spasmodically,
and then put them round Vardalek's neck.
This was the only movement he had made for
some time. Vardalek bent down and kissed him
on the lips. I rushed downstairs: and the
priest was sent for ...

COUNT ERIC STENBOCK
'The True Story of a Vampire', 1894

Left: Ganymede, Coreggio, Kunsthistorisches Museum, Vienna
Above: Ganymede, Rubens, Fürst Schwarzenberg Collection, Vienna

My Own Boy

*Your sonnet is quite lovely, and it is a
marvel that those red rose-leaf lips of
yours should have been made no less for
music of song than for madness of kisses.
Your slim gilt soul walks between passion
and poetry. I know Hyacinthus, whom Apollo
loved so madly, was you in Greek days ...*

OSCAR WILDE

*to Lord Alfred Douglas, January, 1893
Used in evidence at the Wilde v Queensbury trial
and the subsequent Regina v Wilde trials, 1895*

Right: An Elegant Young Man from 'L'Assiette au Beurre', 1909, M. Vadasz

Above: Nijinsky's faun costume from 'L'Après Midi d'un Faune'
by Debussy, Bibliothèque Nationale de France, Paris

Oh, lover
Why don't we realize
that no affair is forever?
Why is it that,
after coupling with
someone new,
we allow those sometimes
soft deep things inside
to spill free
—creating feelings
it would be better
if we could hide?

PAUL KELLER

1969

22

Above: The Mirror of Love, Aubrey Beardsley

Left: Contents page from 'Salome', Aubrey Beardsley

*They slept, four heads to the centre pole of the
tent. Aaron's face inches away, asleep, breathing
evenly. Impossible for Tim to sleep. He had seen
his love undress and hoped desperately his own eyes
had gone unnoticed. Last summer's suntan on Aaron
was still evident, but white where he'd worn his
bathing trunks. Almost white hair on the golden legs.
There was only one possible answer in the circumstances,
he told himself. Aaron, stretch out a hand and touch
me, put your hand where mine is.*

DAVID REES
'In the Tent', 1979

Above: Two Boys in a Pool, Hollywood, David Hockney
Left: *Detail*, copyright David Hockney, 1965

Gaveston:

I must have wanton poets, pleasant wits,
Musicians, that with touching of a string
may draw the pliant king which way I please.
Music and poetry is his delight;
Therefore I'll have Italian masks by night,
Sweet speeches, comedies and pleasing shows;
And in the day, when he shall walk abroad,
Like sylvan nymphs my pages shall be clad;
My men, like satyrs grazing on the lawns,
Shall with their goat-feet dance, the antic hay.

CHRISTOPHER MARLOW
'Edward the Second', Act 1, Scene 9, 16th century

Above: Henry Percy, 9th Earl of Northumberland,
Nicholas Hilliard, Fitzwilliam Museum, University of Cambridge
Right: Henry Percy, Nicholas Hilliard, Rijksmuseum, Amsterdam

He moves Titanic 'mid the strife of games,
So fleet of foot, so sure of eye, so glorious,
With stately youth, and beauty which enflames
Desire for him, thus splendidly victorious.
O come, dear Love, come touch his hand,
And make my lover understand.

REGINALD BRETT,
2nd Viscount Esher, 'Briseis' 1893

Left: Illustration for 'Ballet Jeux' starring Nijinsky, Montenegro, 1914
Above: Nijinsky in 'Giselle', Georges Barbier, 1913

Have you learn'd lessons only of those who admired you,
and were tender with you, and stood aside for you?
Have you not learn'd great lessons from those who reject
you, and brace themselves against you? or treat you with
contempt, or dispute passage with you?

WALT WHITMAN
'Stronger Lessons', 1888

Above: I Will Sing a Song of Companionship
Right: When He Whom I Love Travels With Me,
both by Margaret C. Cook in Whitman's 'Leaves of Grass', 1913

Boys
  Bursting the surface of the ebony pond.
Flashes
  Of swimmers carving thro' the sparkling cold.
Fleshes
  Gleaming with wetness to the morning gold.

WILFRED OWEN
'From My Diary', July 1914'

Above: Ruby, Gold and Malachite, Forbes Magazine Collection
Left: Lovers of the Sun, Guildhall Art Gallery,
Corporation of London, both by Henry Scott Tuke

If I could paint you, friend, as you stand there,
Guard of the goal, defensive, open-eyed,
Watching the tortured bladder slide and glide
Under the twinkling feet; arms bare, head bare,
The breeze a-tremble through crow-tufts of hair;
Red-brown in face, and ruddier having spied
A wily foeman breaking from the side;
Aware of him, – of all else unaware:
If I could limn you, as you leap and fling
Your weight against his passage like a wall;
Clutch him, and collar him, and rudely cling
For one brief moment till he falls – you fall:
My sketch would have what Art can never give –
Sinew and breath and body; it would live.

EDWARD CRACROFT LEFROY
'A Football Player', 19th century

Previous page: Will He Do It?, George Elgar Hicks, Private Collection

He was young; and despite his all but fully developed frame, in aspect looked even younger than he really was. This was owing to a lingering adolescent expression in the as yet smooth face, all but feminine in purity of natural complexion, but where, thanks to his sea going, the lily was quite suppressed, and the rose had some ado visibly to flush through the tan.

HERMAN MELVILLE
'Billy Budd', 1924

Above: Sailor – *detail*, Reimonde Kimpe, Whitford & Hughes, London

*I am distressed for thee, my brother
Jonathan: very pleasant hast thou been
unto me: thy love to me was wonderful,
passing the love of women*

DAVID AND JONATHAN
'The Second Book of Samuel', Chapter 1, Verse 26

Above: Man with Glove, Titian, Louvre, Paris
Right: The Fine Man, Titian,
Kunsthistorisches Museum, Vienna

*'Tiny and Tibi! Enough.' The intervention came from
the full-voiced Christobal, a youngster of fifteen, with
soft, peach-textured cheeks, and a tongue never far
away. Considered an opportunist, he was one of the
six dancing-boys of the cathedral.*

*'Order!' Felix enjoined anew. Finely sensitive as to his
prerogative, the interference of his colleague was apt
to vex him. He would be trying to clip an altar pose
next. Indeed, it was a matter of scandal already, how
he was attempting to attract attention, in influential
places, by the unnecessary undulation of his loins ...*

RONALD FIRBANK
'Concerning the Eccentricities of Cardinal Pirelli', 1926

You, proud curve-lipped youth, with brown sensitive face,
Why, suddenly, as you sat there on the grass, did you turn full upon me those twin black eyes of yours,
With gaze so absorbing so intense, I a strong man trembled and was faint?

EDWARD CARPENTER
'Towards Democracy', 1881-1882

Above: The Lover Proud, Simeon Solomon, The Maas Gallery, London
Left: Lutenist, Caravaggio, State Hermitage, St. Petersburg

Now his lovely cap is treated like a lover: off it goes!
Next his belt the boy unbuckles; down it falls,
and at his toes
All the growing heap of garments buds and
blossoms like a rose.
Last of all his shirt comes flying. Ah, I tremble to disclose
How the shell came off the almond,
how the lily showed its face,
How I saw a silver mirror taken flashing from its case.

JAMES ELROY FLECKER
'The Hammam Name', 20th century

Above and right: Illustration by Ian Beck in 'The Joy of Gay Sex'

*I never yet cast a true affection on a woman; but
I have loved my friend as I do virtue, my soul, my
God ... I love my friend before myself, and yet
methinks I do not love him enough ...*

SIR THOMAS BROWNE
'Religio Medici', 1642

Left: St. Sebastian, Antonio Pollainolo, National Gallery, London
Above: The Dying Slave, Michelangelo, Louvre, Paris

I loved you, so I drew these tides of men into my hands
and wrote my will across the sky in stars
To earn you Freedom, the seven pillared worthy house,
that your eyes might be shining for me
When we came.

T.E. LAWRENCE
'To S.A.'
'Seven Pillars of Wisdom', 1926

Above: T.E. Lawrence
Right: Mukheymer

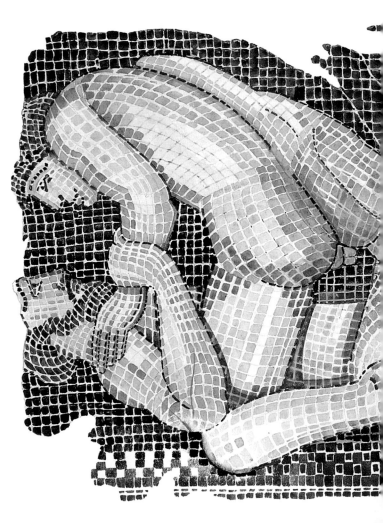

If all complying, thou would'st grant
Thy lovely eyes to kiss, my fair,
Long as I pleased' oh! I would plant
Three hundred thousand kisses there.

Nor could I even then refrain,
Nor satiate leave that fount of blisses,
Tho' thicker than autumnal grain
Should be our growing crop of kisses.

CATULLUS

'To Juventius', 1st century B.C.

(translated Hon. J. Lamb)

Above and left: Illustration by Ian Beck in 'The Joy of Gay Sex'

49

Love a woman?
You're an ass!
Tis a most insipid
passion
To choose out for your
happiness
The silliest part of God's
creation

JOHN WILMOT
Earl of Rochester, 17th century

Right: Boy and Horse, marble relief from
Hadrian's Villa, Tivoli

Above: Bronze figure of David, Donatello,
Bargello Florence

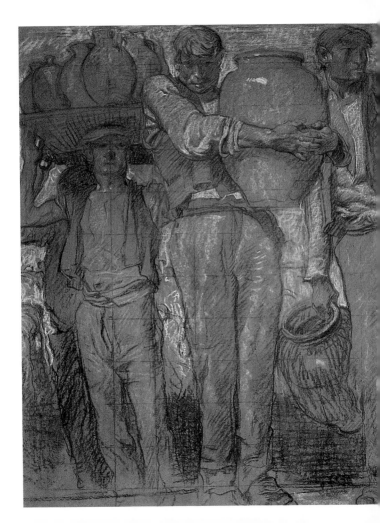

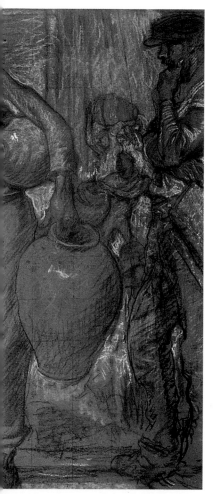

*Rhymes on rhymes fair
meaning carry,
Thoughts to think bring
deeper joy;
Sing to other folk, but tarry
Silent with thy serving boy.*

JOHANN GOETHE
17th century

Left: The Potters,
Sir Frank Brangwyn,
The Fine Art Society, London

A Grecian lad, as I hear tell,
One that many loved in vain,
Looked into a forest well
And never looked away again.
There, when the turf in springtime flowers,
With downward eye and gazes sad,
Stands amid the glancing showers
A jonquil, not a Grecian lad.

A.E. HOUSEMAN
'A Shropshire Lad', 1896

Above: Nijinsky in 'L'Après-midi d'un Faune', Georges Barbier, 1913
Right: Nijinsky in 'Swan Lake', Georges Barbier, 1913

O say, and again repeat, fair, fair—and still
I will say it –
How fair, my friend, and good to see, thou art;
On pine or oak or wall they name I do not blazon –
Love has too deeply graved it in my heart.

Epigram

'The Greek Anthology'

Above: Illustration by Ian Beck in

'The Joy of Gay Sex'

*Quite other things were going through Birkin's mind.
Suddenly he saw himself confronted with another
problem – the problem of love and eternal conjunction
between two men. Of course this was necessary – it
had been a necessity inside himself all his life – to
love a man purely and fully. Of course he had been
loving Gerald all along, and all along denying it.*

D.H. LAWRENCE
'Women in Love', 1921

Above: Zeus and Eagle abducting Ganymede,
Archaeological Museum, Ferrara
Right: Greek Vase Painting with Dancing Faun

Posh was, in Fitzgerald's own words, 'a man of the finest Saxon type, with a complexion, vif, male et flamboyant, blue eyes, a nose less than Roman, more than Greek, and strictly auburn hair that woman might sigh to possess.'

A.C. BENSON
'Edward Fitzgerald', 1905

Strolling along the shore towards them came a strange and beautiful figure, a boy of seventeen or eighteen, naked but for a pair of tattered breeches, with his skin tanned to iodine brown by the sun and the sea. A wreath of ivy and wild-vine was twined in his yellow hair, and to his mouth he held a reed-pipe on which he blew squealing sounds ...

E.F. BENSON
'The Inheritor', 1930

Above: The Triumph of Bacchus – *detail*,
Diego Velasquez, Museo del Prado, Madrid

Above: The Young Bacchus, Michelangelo Caravaggio,
Uffizi Gallery, Florence

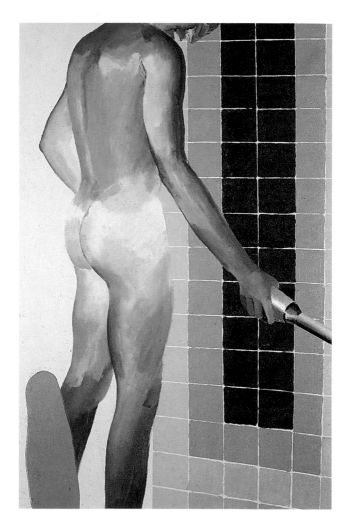

'You are beautiful,' Rolf said very softly. 'Come.' He patted the bed. 'Do you mind if I turn out the light?' Paul asked. Rolf shrugged. 'I don't mind. But I would love to be able to watch you.' Paul gazed at Rolf. 'I'd feel better in the dark,' he said. 'Very well,' Rolf nodded. Paul padded on his bare feet across the room, acutely aware that Rolf was observing every portion of his naked body ...

ROBIN MAUGHAM
'Enemy!', 1981

Left: Boy About to Take a Shower, David Hockney,
copyright David Hockney, 1964
Above: Naked Man With His Friend, Lucien Freud

PHOTOGRAPHIC ACKNOWLEDGEMENTS

Front cover: Bridgeman Art Library /Victoria & Albert Museum.
Back flap: AKG London.
The picture on page 17 is reproduced by courtesy of
The Trustees of the Victoria & Albert Museum/photo: Sara Hodges.
AKG London 8, 18, 19, 38, 39, 40, 60, /Erich Lessing 3;
Bridgeman Art Library /Bargello, Florence 50, /Bibliothèque Nationale
de France, Paris 20, /The Fine Art Society, London 10, 52/53,
/Fitzwilliam Museum, University of Cambridge 26,
/Forbes Magazine Collection 32, /Galleria degli Uffizi, Florence 61,
/Galleria dell'Accademia, Venice 1, /Giraudon/Louvre 6/7,
/Guildhall Art Gallery, Corporation of London 33, /Louvre 45,
/The Maas Gallery, London 41, /National Gallery, London 44,
/Private Collection 11, 24, 25, 34/35, 62, 63,
/Rijksmuseum, Amsterdam 27, /Victoria & Albert Museum 12, 16, 23,
/Whitford & Hughes, London 37;
C M Dixon 50/51;
E.T. Archive 28, 29, 54, 55, 58, 59;
Mary Evans Picture Library 21, 22, 30, 31;
Werner Forman Archive /Egyptian Museum, Cairo 4;
Reed International Books Ltd 46, 47.